BEL1
THE BIG EASY

By

ALICIA LANE DUTTON

Cast of Characters (6-9F)(2M)

Celeste: (40 - 60) a little Hippie-ish, digs Yoga but belongs to the Country Club

Bree: (40 - 60) a little uppity, very fashion conscious

Regina: (40 - 60) cares about her friends not her appearance

Catherine: (40 - 60) a little uptight, career minded

Mary Grace: (40 - 60) hates her mother-in-law, loves Google

Bobbi: (20 - 80) Waffle Barn Waitress

Cherry: (40 - 70) owner of the Lah Tee Dah Day Spa

Thibaut: (40 — 60) owns Cajun Critters Swamp Tour

Blaise: (20 - 70) owns Ball Gowns by Blaise, flamboyant

VooDoo Priestess: (20 - 70) a VooDoo Priestess

Marie: a Merry Maid (20 — 70)

Waiter/Parade Participant: (20-40) waiter at The Old Absinthe House/Dancing parade guy

Multiple Role Suggestions:
Bobbi/Cherry/VooDoo Priestess/Marie
Blaise/Parade Participant/Waiter

ORIGINATING CAST

Celeste – Tracy McCartney
Bree – Alicia Lane Dutton
Regina – Quincy Vidrine
Mary Grace – Malori Byrd Giannaris
Catherine – Marilyn Gibson
Thibaut – Joe Wild
Blaise/Waiter – Dylan Brocato
Cherry – Saylor Leake
VooDoo Priestess/Bobbi/Marie – Tammi Scales

Belles Take the Big Easy was first produced in Natchez, Mississippi at The Storyville Cabaret and Dinner Theater. The show was directed by Alicia Lane Dutton.

One vignette is used for the Waffle Barn/Café Du Monde/Bacchus Ball/Absinthe House by changing the table cloth and hanging a panel with different signs/covers. The Lah Tee Dah Day Spa and the French Quarter Flat double with the use of chair/sofa covers and different art.

ACT ONE
Scene 1

CELESTE is sitting in the driver's seat of a car. The car can be as basic or detailed as you'd like. There must be two seats in front and three raised in the back so we can see the occupants later. BREE, wearing a patterned dress and sunglasses, enters with a rolling suitcase.

CELESTE
Are those really your traveling clothes? Surely you could at least slum it while we're in the car.
BREE
I am slumming it. This is last year's pattern.

BREE puts her suitcase in the "trunk" and gets in the front seat. CATHERINE enters with a rolling bag, matching make up case, and duffel. She has on a scarf tied almost like an ascot. She waves to the ladies and spends a long time in the back unseen "arranging" the bags.

CELESTE
What are you doing back there?
CATHERINE
I'm arranging the luggage in a spatial distribution that is most efficient.
CELESTE
You're what?
CATHERINE gets in the back seat annoying Bree in the process.
CATHERINE
We are going to have five ladies in one car with all their luggage. We have to be careful

how we stack things so that we'll have enough
room.

BREE

Don't look at me. I'm not the one who brought
three bags. I learned my lesson after my Louis
Vuitton took flight out of the back end of
that hybrid car truck thing you had when we
went to Vegas.

CELESTE

It was an environmentally friendly flexicab.

BREE

Well, whatever that eyesore was, somehow you
thought it was my fault that my bag flew out
and not the way you took that curve.

CELESTE

You brought seven pieces of luggage! It was
Vegas. How many items of clothing does one
need? It was so hot I would have gone naked
had they let me.

BREE

You actually would have.

CELESTE

Yes, I would have Miss Prude.

BREE

Hippie Wannabee.

CATHERINE

Can we not relive the Vegas incident again?

BREE

That's easy for you to say. Your bandoulière
did not take flight into the desert somewhere
between the airport and the triple threat
alien welcome center, cafe, and BROTHEL.

CELESTE

It was good thinking to have the girls who
were in between clients wait tables. Now
that's efficiency.

*MARY GRACE ENTERS. She waves to the ladies and
places her bag in the back.*

BREE
I love the new fountain, Mary Grace. I saw it
on my way to the gym Thursday night.

MARY GRACE makes her way into the back seat,

MARY GRACE
You do, huh? Tell that to Lillian. She said it
looks like something a nouveau riche lottery
winner would put in front of a double wide.
BREE
I do not know how you put up with that evil
mother-in-law of yours.
MARY GRACE
Oh, I just smile and think about the fact that
any riche is good riche and after she kicks
the bucket Kenneth and I will be a lot more
riche. So I just don't let Lillian bother me.
I used to let it bother me and I actually had
contemplated whispering to her on her deathbed
that my three children were really compliments
of my favorite bag boy at Piggly Wiggly, kind
of like a Braveheart moment, but I'm past
that.

*BREE and CELESTE look at one another a little
scared of MARY GRACE for a moment.*

CELESTE
OK. Time to go get Regina.
CATHERINE
She couldn't meet at the park and ride like
the rest of us?
CELESTE
It's on the way. She said she needed a little
more beauty sleep. You know she's a night owl.
CATHERINE
She's only a night owl because she stays up

eating Cheez-Its and binge-watching raunchy Net Flix Movies.

BREE

She claims it's necessary research for work.

CELESTE

Why did we ever let her invest in that one nine hundred number?

MARY GRACE

As Regina says...

ALL

It pays the bills!

CELESTE

Who would have ever thought you could make so much money yelling at men?

MARY GRACE

I yell at Kenneth all the time and it hasn't made me a dime.

CELESTE

(in a sultry voice)

Maybe you're just not doing it right.

MARY GRACE

Apparently not.

ACT ONE
Scene 2

*REGINA is lying in a bed under the covers,
wearing a night mask. Her phone rings. She
fumbles for it then answers it.*

REGINA
I'm ready.

*REGINA yanks off the covers revealing she is
fully clothed including flip flops. She
stumbles around, removes the nightmask, and
grabs the handle of her suitcase. Her hair is
crazy. She approaches the car and waves to the
ladies. She disappears behind the car for a
moment but reappears still with her suitcase.*

CATHERINE
Why didn't you put your bag in the trunk?
REGINA
I didn't want to mess up that luggage Jenga
game you've got going on back there.

CATHERINE gets out of the car.

CATHERINE
Give me that.

*CATHERINE takes REGINA'S bag and heads to the
back of the car.*

REGINA
Maybe you can relax when we get to New
Orleans.

CATHERINE reappears without the bag.

CATHERINE
I am relaxed.

REGINA
You have on an ascot.

CATHERINE
It's not an ascot, it's a scarf.

REGINA
No one who is headed to the French Quarter
would wear an ascot OR a scarf, unless they're
uptight.

*CATHERINE pouts, removes the scarf and hands
it (or tosses it across "the car") to REGINA
and gets into the back of the car. REGINA
smiles, puts on sunglasses smugly, and gets
into the back, obnoxiously bumping into
everyone. She plops into the seat.*

REGINA
Goodbye Downton Abbey, hello New Orleans!

*REGINA swings the scarf like a lasso above her
head and lets it fly toward the back of the
car.*

ACT ONE
Scene 3

The ladies are still in the car. They clearly have been riding a while. They are napping, doing nails, playing on phone etc.

REGINA
I need a break.
CELESTE
What?! We've already stopped to pee three times and once to get ice cream. You're like a toddler.
REGINA
I've had three toddlers so now I pee like one. There's a Waffle Barn! Pull in! Pull in!

The ladies exit the car and seat themselves in a circular booth (or round table with chairs).

REGINA
If I were ever forced to eat at one restaurant for the rest of my life it would be Waffle Barn. They have steaks, salads, breakfast all day.. They have pies, everything.

BOBBIE enters and heads to the booth.

BOBBIE
Good morning! Welcome to Waffle Barn. What can I get for y'all?
REGINA
I'll have a glass of baby juice, a double order of hashbrowns scattered, smothered, covered, chunked, and country. And Adam and Eve on a raft.

BOBBIE doesn't flinch and writes it down.

BOBBIE
And what can I get for you, hon?
CATHERINE
(to REGINA)
Adam and Eve on a raft?
REGINA
Two eggs on toast.
CATHERINE
Why didn't you just say two eggs on toast?
REGINA
Because it's fun. You should try it sometime.
CELESTE
I'll take a veggie omelette.
REGINA
Boooring!!!
MARY GRACE
I'll have a pecan waffle.
CATHERINE
I'll have two eggs over medium and an order of
bacon. Or should I say something like two
chicken littles with a porky pig?
REGINA
That's the spirit!
BREE
I'll have a cup of mud, blonde with sand, a
heart attack on a rack, and a Noah's boy.
BOBBIE
Coming right up!
*BOBBIE flits off leaving the others staring at
BREE.*
CELESTE
What's a Noah's boy?
BREE
Ham of course. I may or may not have worked in
a diner when I was younger. And, I may or may
not have been crowned Miss Interstate 55 Exit
29A Waffle Barn Queen. How do you think I paid
for nursing school?

MARY GRACE

Our Bree working in a diner. Who knew?

BREE

Practiced my talent song to the Jukebox. Louisiana Woman, Mississippi Man. Brought the house down or at least the Waffle Barn that is.

CATHERINE

Who knew we were in the presence of a queen?

BREE

Met my Ronald on a slow Friday night. I became his Louisiana woman and he became my Mississippi man.

CATHERINE

You mean to tell us you met your doctor husband at a diner and not at the hospital?

BREE

Diners are the great equalizers of society. You can meet all kinds of folks in a diner.

MARY GRACE

It's true. Look at us, a booth full of ladies from Flovilla, Alabama taking off to The Big Easy to experience Mardi Gras before we kick the bucket.

CATHERINE

Mary Grace, can we just say to check it off our bucket list?

MARY GRACE

If that makes you feel better about doing it before we kick the bucket.

REGINA

Did y'all know FEMA rates disasters by whether or not Waffle Barn is open?

CATHERINE

You've got to be kidding.

REGINA

I'm not kidding. It's called The Waffle Barn Index. After a big hurricane or whatever if

Waffle Barn is open and serving their full
menu, it's code green. If it's on a limited
menu, it's code yellow. If Waffle Barn is
closed, it is serious. That's code RED.
They'll call out the National Guard without
even having seen the damage.
BREE
Lucky for us it's code green and you know what
that means!..... Jukebox time!

*BREE heads toward a jukebox offstage singing a
snippet of Conway Twitty's Louisiana Woman,
Mississippi Man.*

ACT ONE
Scene 4

All five ladies are back in the car napping, listening to headphones etc.

BREE
Oo! Oo! Look at that billboard! The La Tee Dah Day Spa. Voted the best day spa in Bayou George, Mississippi.

MARY GRACE
It's probably the only day spa in Bayou George, Mississippi.

CATHERINE
Who names a town Bayou George?

REGINA
Somebody fun, that's who, by George!

BREE
I don't care if it's Bayou George or Bayou Fred, Mississippi. All I know is that it has a day spa and we could probably all use a little break. We'll still get to New Orleans in time for supper. Come on ladies let's treat ourselves.

CELESTE
Treat ourselves? I kind of thought heading to New Orleans on a girls' trip was treating ourselves.

MARY GRACE
Bree may have a point, Celeste. There's nothing wrong with pampering ourselves a little. I was so busy helping plan the Pig Jig I haven't had time to go by Fancy Fingers this week.

CATHERINE
Look, I don't want to end up at the bottom of some swamp in a backwoods Mississippi town. Can't we wait until we get to a rest area to stop? We can pamper ourselves with a trip to

the toilet and a few nice vending machine
items.
REGINA
You think a rest area is going to be safer
than a Bayou George, Mississippi day spa?
MARY GRACE
I'm not worried. I'm carrying.
CATHERINE
Carrying what?
BREE/REGINA
Me too.

*MARY GRACE, BREE, and REGINA pull out handguns
from their purses.*

BREE
(Points with her gun)
There's the exit! 14B!
CELESTE
I can't believe I'm doing this, but we are on
vacation.
BREE
That's the spirit!
CELESTE
Exiting.

*Everyone leans in the same direction as the
car "exits" the interstate.*

MARY GRACE
Oo! It's pink!
CATHERINE
It's cinder block.
MARY GRACE
Cinder block is just like cellulite. It looks
much better in pink.
CATHERINE
What?

MARY GRACE

Why do you think strip clubs all have pink lighting? It makes the girls' skin look flawless.

CATHERINE

How would you know about lighting in a strip club, Mary Grace?

MARY GRACE

Ladies, Catherine has evidently never been in a strip club.

CELESTE/REGINA/BREE

Really?

CATHERINE

You all have?

CELESTE

I forgot she wasn't in our circle of friends when we went to Swinging Richard's for MiMi MacIntyre's fourth bachelorette party.

CATHERINE

Swinging Richard's?

REGINA

It's a coed strip joint near the county line. They've got female and male strippers. You can have a bachelor's or a bachelorette party there or I guess anything in between if you're confused about your gender, I guess.

BREE

Can we go in already? I can't wait to check out The Lah Tee Dah Day Spa, ladies!

ACT ONE
Scene 5

The La Tee Dah Day Spa. CATHERINE, REGINA,
CELESTE, BREE, and MARY GRACE enter the spa.
The front counter is tufted in hot pink
leather and lined with faux zebra fur. From
the back, CHERRY, a pretty, older woman in a
velour track suit with bouffant hair enters.
She has on a nametag that says Cherry.

BREE
Hi there! Cherry, is it? We're on our way to
The Big Easy and we want to look and feel our
very best on our vacation.
CHERRY
You have come to the right place. Would any of
you ladies like a mimosa?
ALL
I would!
CHERRY
Five mimosas coming up! Feel free to browse
our menu cards.

CHERRY exits. BREE passes menu cards to all
the ladies and keeps one for herself.

CELESTE
What is a prickly pear wrap?
REGINA
I think the bigger question is what is
Vajazzling? It kind of sounds like putting
your little princess down in a tub filled with
fizzy water.
MARY GRACE
Your little princess?
CELESTE
The aromatherapy massage looks enticing,
especially after driving half the day.

CHERRY enters with a tray of six mimosas (one for her).

CHERRY
Here we are! Have you ladies had a chance to look at the menu?
CELESTE
I was thinking about the aromatherapy massage.
CHERRY
Oooo, good choice. Our masseuse Brigitta has strong hands and you'll feel like a mushy biscuit covered in gravy after you're done.

CELESTE looks slightly frightened.

BREE
I have a few questions.
CHERRY
Shoot.
BREE
I'm extremely curious about the Vajazzling service.
CHERRY
Oh, the Vajazzling! We used to have Vajazzling on the Vault menu only, but it was so popular we moved it right on to our La Tee Dah menu. It's basically like bedazzling your hoo-ha.
REGINA
I think she's referring to your little princess, Bree.
CATHERINE
Piercing your princess with rhinestones?!
CHERRY
Oh no, honey! That sounds painful! We don't do piercings at La Tee Dah. I frankly think it's kinda tacky. With Vajazzling, little crystals are applied to your.....little princess with an adhesive backing, after a Hollywood wax of course.

MARY GRACE
Every year my Nana gives me one of those
crystal figurines for Christmas. Next year
I'll just say, Nana, I want the crystal
butterfly, but not the little statuette kind,
I want its wings spread right across my
hoo-ha!

MARY GRACE takes a long swig of her mimosa.

BREE
And what exactly is Naked Tan?
CHERRY
Nekkid tan? That's the brand of spray tan we
use. We used to use Turbo Tan but some of the
ladies thought it made them look jaundiced
(jaundice is whispered loudly).
REGINA
Since Bree seems to be finished with her
little spa inquisition, I'd like to know what
The Vault Menu is. It says The Vault Menu is
available upon request. I'm officially
requesting it.

*CHERRY reaches behind the counter and takes
out small black cards with red writing.*

CHERRY
OK. Y'all asked for it. *(CHERRY passes out
cards.)* The Vault is a bunker room underneath
the spa. We really needed to expand but the
only place we could go was down into an old
tornado safe room. We decided to put our more
sensitive, personal services down there.
REGINA
Python massage.
CELESTE
Vattooing?

REGINA

I think they mean tattooing your-

CELESTE

Little Princess!! Yes, I get it Regina but good Lord!

MARY GRACE

Candle Waxing?

CATHERINE

A Spa Spank?

BREE

Cherry, with all due respect you seem to be in somewhat of a small, rural town. Do you have much Vault type clientele?

CHERRY

Oh yes, Honey! I know Bayou George isn't exactly a bustling metropolis, but we get loads of folks on their way to the beach, or to New Orleans like you ladies, on their way to gamble in Biloxi, or folks who are on their way to catch cruise ships. We even have alternative life clubs from Atlanta come in on field trips. Brigitta and her partner Ilka oversee all The Vault activities. Our python massage is performed by their Ball Python, Lucille. It's all the rage in Europe and now right here in the Delta!

CELESTE

I think I'll just have a massage which is, I guess, the missionary position equivalent of the offerings here at The Lah Tee Dah.

CHERRY

I'll get Brigitta to come up from the vault!

ACT ONE
Scene 6

Lah Tee Dah Day Spa. CELESTE, MARY GRACE,
REGINA, CATHERINE, and BREE are in matching
aqua terry robes. MARY GRACE has cucumbers on
her eyes and is holding a mimosa. The other
ladies are in various states of "spa-ness";
wrapped hair, drying nails, etc. CHERRY is
also holding a mimosa.

CATHERINE
This was the best idea you've had in a long
time, Bree.
CHERRY
Y'all are lucky you came today. This is
normally the day The First Hope of the Last
Chance Ladies' Bible Study comes. They had to
cancel because they had their Soul Sisters
Searching for Salvation Conference this
week.
MARY GRACE
A Ladies' Bible Study group meets at The Lah
Tee Dah Day Spa?
CHERRY
Every week. All the ladies from The First Hope
of the Last Chance Baptist Church are clients.
BREE
I would be so right with the Lord if I was in
that Bible study group.
CHERRY
The motto of The First Hope of the Last Chance
Ladies' Bible Study Group is... "studying the
word of the Lord while taking care of his
temple."
REGINA
Amen! (*She lifts her glass*)

CELESTE
Looks like you've got a fine business here,
Cherry.
CHERRY
La Tee Dah is my pride and joy. Being raised
in Bayou George, I'd see the tourists come
through on a final stop for gas or the
restroom. They'd have their luggage racks
full, all excited about their vacation. About
the only vacation my family went on was when
we'd picnic alongside the Mississippi River
and we'd have spam sandwiches and cantaloupe
wedges. Daddy couldn't afford too many days
away from work with a wife and seven kids
to feed. But now I'm doing just fine and I
even have my own condo at the beach so if a
van load of sissies wants to have a python
squeeze on them until they're relaxed then so
be it.

CATHERINE holds up her mimosa for a toast.

CATHERINE
To Cherry and The La Tee Dah!
BREE/MARY GRACE/REGINA/CELESTE
Here! Here!
CHERRY
Now, thanks to The Lah Tee Dah, y'all are all
ready for The Big Easy!

ACT ONE
Scene 7

CELESTE, MARY GRACE, REGINA, CATHERINE, and
BREE are back in the car. REGINA is reading a
book.

REGINA
Mmmmmm... *(giggles a little)* Uhhh Huhhh
(seductively)
Mmm huh hummm mmm mmm.
MARY GRACE
Are you reading smut over there?
REGINA
It's not smut, it's research.
BREE
You need to do research on how to yell at men
over the phone and tell them you're going to
beat their butts?
MARY GRACE
You could just record me yelling at my kids,
especially after Jackson cut off his sister's
ponytail. I'm still trying to get over it.
CELESTE
Oh Mary Grace, Emma Jane's hair looks good in
that pixie cut.
MARY GRACE
You and I both know Emma Jane's got ears like
a Lord of the Rings Elf. I'm praying Jackson
doesn't lob any more of her hair off before it
reaches the tops of her ears, bless her heart.
REGINA
Mmmmm Hmmmmm..Tell him girl! That's exactly
what that whip's for!
CELESTE
Could you do your research silently? It's
distracting, and since we're going across the
world's longest bridge I need to focus and

make sure we don't all go swimming in Lake
Pontchartrain.

CATHERINE

Correction. It used to be the world's longest
bridge but some bridge in China just beat it
out.

MARY GRACE

Those dad gum Chinese. Normally they take our
stuff and make it smaller like computers and
cell phone components. Now they're beating us
out with big stuff.

REGINA

Well, we've got 'em beat on eating utensils.
Ever try to eat Bar B Que with a chopstick?

BREE

Speaking of Bar B Que, are y'all going to help
me and Mary Grace on the Pig Jig Committee
this year?

CELESTE

How many times have I told you, Bree? I'm
happy to help with the Fire Ant Festival
because it actually celebrates one of God's
most hated creatures. I'm not sure why
but...whatever. Anyway, as a vegetarian I
cannot be a party to the exploitation of pigs.

REGINA

For God's sake Celeste, we're not exploiting
them, we're eating them. You act like we're
humiliating them or something.

MARY GRACE

That's true Celeste. It's hard for something
to feel exploited if it's dead.

CELESTE

It's the Pig Jig. At first it sounds innocent
like pigs dancing the polka but in reality,
it's a bunch of people with gazillion dollar
smokers engaging in a contest to see who can
char innocent pigs the best. It's barbaric.

MARY GRACE
It might be Celeste, but it's a boon to Flovilla's economy.

BREE
It's not just about charbroiling delicious swine meat. Don't forget the rides for the kids and the carnival games. You could head up the kids' carnival. You'd never have to see a pig, dead or alive.

CELESTE
But I'd have to see a carnie!

BREE
A what?

REGINA
A Carnie. A politically incorrect name for a traveling carnival employee usually identified by their multiple tats, piercings, or restraining orders filed against them.

CELESTE
A carnie tried to get me to go behind the lobster boy exhibit with him at the state fair one year. Scared the beJesus out of me so I will not be your liaison between the Pig Jig committee and the carnival folks.

BREE
Celeste, I will excuse your vegetarian self, but the rest of you ladies have no excuse to not help out me and Mary Grace.

MARY GRACE
Go ahead and sign me up for the carnival liaison. *(Brandishes her gun)*
I got this.

REGINA
You know I can't help out. Richard only needs to win two more sanctioned Bar B Que contests before he qualifies for the Chillin' and Grillin' Championship in St. Louis. I can't be on the Pig Jig committee or someone might think I'm trying to rig it for Richard.

MARY GRACE

How convenient Regina. That leaves you, Catherine. Since you're an accountant you can be in charge of the score sheets and present the winners using the sealed envelope like the accountants at the Oscars.

CATHERINE

No can do. The last thing I want is to be party to some La La Land/Moonlight debacle. I might accidentally call The Church of Swinetology as the winner when it was really Team Kill It and Grill It. And the last thing I want is a team of rednecks called Kill It and Grill It after me. No Thanks.

CELESTE

Uh oh.

BREE

Uh oh what?

CELESTE

We're really low on gas.

BREE

Don't you have one of those little lights that warns you?

CELESTE

Yes, Bree. I have one of those little lights.

MARY GRACE

I wouldn't be too worried about it. I can go twenty more miles after the little light comes on.

CELESTE

The problem is I'm not sure when the little light came on.

REGINA

Does yours not ding?! Mine dings!

CELESTE

Yes, it dings Regina! However, I didn't hear it! Probably because SOMEONE insisted that I turn up Sweet Home Alabama because according to a certain someone when Lynyrd Skynyrd says turn it up, you do, because if you don't it's some sort of southern mortal sin!

REGINA

Don't be hating on Skynyrd, Celeste! Just because you listen to all that new age mumbo jumbo.

CELESTE

(having a total come apart)

IT RELAXES ME REGINA!

BREE

Now I understand the uh oh.

MARY GRACE

According to Google, after we cross the lake, there's still two miles of bayou to go over before we get to solid ground which translates to a gas station.

CATHERINE

Oh Lord please don't let us break down in a bayou.

BREE

Why not Catherine? The last bayou we were in was Bayou George, Mississippi and they had a day spa!

CATHERINE

That was not a real bayou, Bree! That was a town with a name that was a play on words. A TOWN with solid packed ground, not a marshland full of alligators and snakes.

REGINA

Don't forget wild boars. We smoked a wild boar for the Bacon County Bodacious Butt Bar B Que Contest and won most original flavor last year.

CELESTE

Well, this is just great. We come on our first bucket list trip and because of me we might end up in a bayou being charged by a wild boar.

REGINA
Or eaten by an alligator.
BREE
You're really not helping Regina.
REGINA
Listen, I AM helping. I'm offering options. I
would rather be snatched by an alligator and
rolled under the swamp water until I drowned
not knowing about all that gnawing he'd do on
me later. I'll take that route to my maker
instead of being gored to death by a giant
boar. After all the pigs Richard and I have
smoked and consumed, it would be my worst
nightmare.
CELESTE
Can we stop talking about all the ways to die
in a bayou?! We might not run out of gas and
all this talk will have been completely
futile.

The ladies jerk forward a few times.

BREE
Uh oh.
MARY GRACE
Pull over and get out of the lane! If we cause
a traffic jam on this bridge, we'll die by
Louisiana Cajun with a bad case of road rage.

*CELESTE turns the wheel indicating she is
pulling the car off the side of the road.*

BREE
Put on your hazards. I'll just be a minute.
CELESTE
Where are you going?
BREE
I'm doing something your feminazi ways won't
allow you to do apparently. I'm using what the

good Lord gave me.

BREE gets out of the car and walks around to the driver's side. She pulls her neckline down a little, raises her skirt etc. and stands in a seductive pose.

CELESTE
I can't believe you!
BREE
You know miss, "I am woman hear me roar," sometimes actions speak louder than words to get us rescued from this bridge. Or, you can start walking. In a few miles you'll be at the end of the bridge and the beginning of the alligator infested waters of the Bayou Sauvage Wildlife Area according to the map.

CELESTE contemplates this. She then jumps out of the car and joins BREE trying to look seductive.

CELESTE
Oo! I think that truck is slowing down!
BREE
He's pulling over!
CELESTE
Get back in the car!

CELESTE and BREE race to get back into the car.

MARY GRACE
Lock the doors!

THIBAUT enters and approaches Celeste on the driver's side.

THIBAUT
Good afternoon. Name's Thibaut. (Pronounced
TEE-BOE.)
ALL
Good afternoon, Hi there etc.
CELESTE
Hi, Thibaut. I'm Celeste. This is Bree,
Regina, Mary Grace, and Catherine.
THIBAUT
Nice to meet you ladies.
REGINA
I can assure you the pleasure's all mine.
THIBAUT
It doesn't look like you're running hot.
REGINA
(*Fanning herself*)
Oh, we're running hot alright.
THIBAUT
Excuse me?
CELESTE
She meant we're not running hot. We're out of
gas.
THIBAUT
I figured. I've got a Jerry Can in the truck
with a few gallons in it. I keep it on hand.
CATHERINE
Clearly not your first rodeo with this little
situation.
REGINA
Ooo..Thibaut the Rod-e-o Cowboy. Do you know
how to use a whip?
CELESTE/BREE/MARY GRACE/CATHERINE
Regina!
REGINA
Here's my card. I'm always looking for
inspiration.

A few of the other ladies push Regina's

*out stretched hand away from Thibaut's
direction.*

CELESTE
I'm so sorry. We checked her out of the..
institution to bring her on her.. final death
wish trip.
THIBAUT
Excuse me?
CATHERINE
She means her.. Make a Wish Trip for mentally
unstable sex perverts.. who are locked up for
their own good.
THIBAUT
(*Backs away nervously*)
I'm just gonna put a little gas in your car so
y'all can be on your way. No need to thank me.

*THIBAUT exits, gets gas can and re-enters
"putting the gas in the side of the car."
Looking suspiciously toward the ladies to
ensure no one gets out of the car.*

CELESTE
My Lord, Regina! Normally people out of gas on
the side of the road should be scared of a
stranger approaching, but in this case we
managed to turn the tables.
MARY GRACE
Look at him. He can't get that gas in this car
fast enough. He's as nervous as a minnow in a
bass pond.
CELESTE
Well, I wonder why?! He thinks there's an
escaped sex pervert in the car. What were you
thinking Catherine?
CATHERINE
I'm sorry Miss, she's on her DEATH WISH TRIP!

THIBAUT finishes, and waves as he exits, nervously.

REGINA
I don't know about y'all, but this supposed sex maniac is ready to get over this bridge and into the French Quarter! I need a drink. Drive on James! Wuh Tow!
(Making whip crack noise.)

ACT ONE
Scene 8

REGINA, CELESTE, CATHERINE, BREE, AND MARY
GRACE enter the living area of an opulent
French Quarter Flat. The ladies are each
holding a mixed drink, purse, and dragging a
rolling suitcase.

REGINA
I like this plan of striking things off a list
before we kick the bucket! To New Orleans!
Cheers!
CATHERINE
For heaven's sake, striking things off the
BUCKET LIST. When y'all say kick the bucket it
sounds like a dreadful foreboding.
MARY GRACE
It is a dreadful foreboding, Catherine.
Everybody's going to kick the bucket sooner or
later.
CATHERINE
True, but we don't have to keep referring to
our list as that.
BREE
I like calling it that. It's like a kick in
the pants to have fun before you kick the
bucket.
CATHERINE
Please, Bree!
CELESTE
She's right. There's more of a sense of
urgency about striking things off the list.
It's easy to procrastinate about doing the
things on a bucket list, but start calling it
a kick the bucket list and it helps get things
moving.
BREE
Exactly! My list is long so we've got to keep

up the momentum ladies. I'm all about having as much fun as possible before I die.

CELESTE

Really?! We couldn't tell with the detour to the La Tee Dah Day Spa on the way to New Orleans.

BREE

You're welcome!

MARY GRACE

This place is something.

REGINA

I feel like a madam and all of you are my girls.

CATHERINE

What?!

REGINA

Nothin'.

BREE

Yeah, I think I'd call this design style, contemporary French Bordello.

CELESTE

It's classic New Orleans French Quarter and we're lucky to be here. Blaise got it for us for free.

MARY GRACE

Free! That's my favorite style.

REGINA

Blaise?

BREE

Who or what may I ask is Blaise?

CELESTE

Blaise is the designer I'm featuring on my new web series.

REGINA

A toast! To Blaise! And free flats!

MARY GRACE

The night is young Regina. You've been finding any excuse to make a toast. You'd better ease up.

BREE
Yeah, you made a toast to the cross walk
giving us the go signal.
CATHERINE
And don't forget we drank a toast to the fact
that we could openly drink a toast on Bourbon
Street.
REGINA
Another toast! To open container laws!
CELESTE
Blaise told me this place used to be a
convent. The nuns are probably rolling over in
their graves about now.
REGINA
A toast to the nuns!
CELESTE
Regina!
REGINA
Hey! They're Catholic! They imbibe. *(She takes
a swig)*
CATHERINE
I wonder if this place is haunted. New Orleans
is supposed to be the most haunted city in
America.
BREE
Maybe since it used to be a convent, all the
bad spirits have stayed away.
MARY GRACE
(Looking at her phone) According to Google,
this building was a lot of things after it was
a convent.
REGINA
Do tell!
MARY GRACE
It was built as a convent in 1733 but after a
while the nuns and the orphans they took care
of outgrew the building. The famous pirate,

Jean Lafitte, turned it into a warehouse for the things he pillaged. After that it became one of the most famous sporting houses in New Orleans.

BREE

What kind of sport?

REGINA

Probably like a quail plantation.

MARY GRACE

*(Holds her phone closer inspecting what's written)*Oh my! They weren't chasing quail! They were chasing tail! This place WAS a bordello! That's what a sporting house is!

BREE

I told y'all! I know my interior design. I know a bordello when I see it.

MARY GRACE

After the brothel closed down, a voodoo priestess bought the building.

CATHERINE

Nuns, prostitutes, and voodoo priestesses.

REGINA

And now us! A toast!

CELESTE/BREE/MARY GRACE/CATHERINE

No!

CELESTE

Let's go down to Cafe Du Monde and get some coffee and beignets.

REGINA

A toast! To deep fried pastries!

ACT ONE
Scene 9

The ladies are sitting around a table. A Sign reads Cafe du Monde. There are coffee cups and saucers on the table.

REGINA
I never thought I'd find anything that could hold a candle to a Krispy Kreme doughnut but these dang beignets are close!
CATHERINE
Unfortunately for my figure I'm a fan of just about any deep-fried bread with sugar on top; doughnuts, beignets, funnel cakes. If I get anything terminal, I'm installing a deep fryer in my kitchen.
REGINA
A toast! To Catherine who's not going out with a bang, but a sizzle!
CELESTE
Somehow, it's just not the same with a cup of chicory coffee instead of a hurricane but cheers!

CATHERINE takes out a flask.

CATHERINE
Ladies, I know it might seem out of character-
MARY GRACE
You're holding a flask Catherine, that seems VERY out of character.
REGINA
I'm telling you. Once I made her remove that ascot it let the blood start flowing back to her brain. Now Catherine is all aboard the Mardi Gras party train!
CATHERINE
The fact is I have something better to toast

tonight than the fact it's a day that ends in
"Y," Regina.
REGINA
That was a valid excuse.
CATHERINE
Anyway, pass it around ladies. I've been
holding this news in for a week.

*The ladies all add a dash of liquor from the
flask into their coffee cups.*

BREE
Do tell!!
MARY GRACE
Does this have anything to do with "the
incident"?
CATHERINE
You know, you ladies have been referring to
what happened to me as "the incident" for
almost a year now. I am a grown woman. You can
say it and it won't upset me. Besides.. Dick
has been paid back a hundred fold.
MARY GRACE
I knew it had something to do with the
incident! I mean...Dick!
CATHERINE
You remember that little good for nothing
trollop he left me for?
REGINA
The temp?
CATHERINE
Yes, the temp the agency sent to be his
secretary for the day. The same temp that he
kept around for a year even though she can't
type or spell the word cat?!
CELESTE
Wait a minute. You said you weren't going to
get upset.

BREE
Let her get upset. If Dick had done that to me, I'd have whacked him to death with my baton.

MARY GRACE
Baton? I thought you sang for your talent in the pageant.

BREE
I sang AND twirled. At the end I karate chopped a cinder block in half. I wore my black belt around my majorette unitard. I had to show them I was multi-talented.

CATHERINE
I'm sorry. I'm really more excited than upset.

CELESTE
Excited?

REGINA
A toast! Catherine is excited about something.

MARY GRACE
Cut it out.

CATHERINE
It turns out that Amber Lynn, the temp, is going to be full time from now on!

BREE
Full time? What do you mean?

CATHERINE
Turns out Dick is going to be a daddy again!

CELESTE/BREE/MARY GRACE
What?!

CATHERINE
Oh yes, he finally gets ours through college and wham! He has to start over with Amber Lynn.

BREE
How do you know?

CATHERINE
He told me! Called me after about four scotches crying and carrying on. He found her

---

birth control pills at the bottom of the
bathroom garbage can. Lord knows the
last time the trash was taken out. She's as
lazy as a dog in August.

CELESTE

Karma!

CATHERINE

Right here at Cafe du Monde is where it ends.
No more talk of the incident. I've finally
gotten closure.

MARY GRACE

I'm sorry you've had to go through all this.

CATHERINE

Don't feel sorry for me! Let me tell y'all. I
couldn't have wished a better revenge on the
man. Raising a toddler with a dumb lazy wife.
There is a God!

MARY GRACE

You're on Regina!

REGINA

A toast! Finally! To Dick and Amber Lynn's
toddler! May he be wild as a buck and not
sleep through the night - or potty train-
until he's four!

ALL

Here! Here!

ACT ONE
Scene 10

There is a sign that says Cajun Critters Swamp Tours. The "car" has been outfitted around the edges as a boat. A small platform sits to the side where Thibaut, the guide, will stand. A long stick lies beside the platform and is used by Thibaut to guide the boat. BREE, MARY GRACE, CATHERINE, CELESTE and REGINA enter.

BREE
When you said you had a surprise for us I was thinking brunch at Muriel's. (*Dreamily*) Brunch with a... a jazz trio playing while we're sitting on a balcony overlooking Jackson Square... eating shrimp and grits.

MARY GRACE
Yeah. Not driving to the ends of the earth down a dirt road to some place the Deliverance cast would be scared to go.

CELESTE
You guys are so unappreciative. I got us all a Groupon to one of the most highly rated things to do in New Orleans.

CATHERINE
And what exactly is out here in the middle of the woods that is so highly rated?

CELESTE
The Cajun Critters Swamp Tour!

REGINA
(*Somberly and with fear in her eyes, looking out toward the audience*) The boars will come for me. I have murdered countless of their brethren and barbecued them for a few plastic trophies.

THIBAUT enters holding a backpack.

CELESTE

Oh my! It's you.

THIBAUT

I could say the same thing, but I would have to change it to "Oh my, it's Y'ALL."

REGINA

Good morning, cowboy.

CELESTE

We came for the swamp tour. What are you doing here?

THIBAUT

I happen to be the proprietor of the swamp tour.

CELESTE

The Cajun Critters Swamp Tour?

THIBAUT

Yep. That's the one. The one on the sign.

MARY GRACE

She just figured the swamp is so vast that perhaps there were several different swamp tours that might shove off from here, hopefully anyway.

THIBAUT

Nope. I'm afraid y'all are stuck with Cajun Critters.

REGINA

Mr. Thibaut, rodeo cowboy, doesn't sound so bad to me.

CELESTE

Don't start!

REGINA

OK, OK.

THIBAUT

Shall we? We can settle up with the Groupons later. Just..love those Groupons.

CATHERINE

Let's go. I've got a new lease on life. Bring on the gators. I'd rather be chased by a gator

than to think I've got to chase a toddler in
my fifties.
THIBAUT
Excuse me?
CELESTE
Ignore her. She's just happy about Dick.
THIBAUT
Excuse me.
CELESTE
Never mind.

*Everyone takes their place on the "boat" with
Thibaut standing on the small platform on the
edge holding the handle of the tiller steer.*

THIBAUT
Ladies, the first thing we're gonna see are
some alligator snapping turtles resting on
that log up there.
MARY GRACE
My Lord. As if alligators weren't enough, the
Louisiana swamps are full of alligator
turtles?
THIBAUT
They're called alligator snapping turtles
because of their powerful jaws and their
ridged skin which looks like an alligator.
REGINA
I hope this boat is good and watertight.
THIBAUT
It hasn't had any leaks in a while.
MARY GRACE
In a while!
THIBAUT
I'm kidding. The alligator snapping turtle has
a worm like appendage on his tongue. He lies
real still with his worm like appendage
hanging out like a lure. *(He stands still and*

sticks out his tongue.) Then, when the prey gets close enough, he chomps down on it!

CELESTE

Worm like appendage? And laying real still til some food passes his way? He sounds like my ex-husband Earl.

THIBAUT

(Thibaut points)

There! On that log to the right!

REGINA

He's a monster! It's like The Land Before Time!

THIBAUT

That's old Alfred. The wildlife biologists in this area think he's around seventy years old. They can live up to a hundred and twenty and grow to be over two hundred pounds.

BREE

Yeah, he's a whopper. Scary!

THIBAUT

He's pretty docile as long as you don't mess with him. If an alligator snapping turtle is forced to leave its resting spot it will become agitated and very aggressive.

CELESTE

Old Alfred sounds more like Earl all the time.

THIBAUT

I don't know how many ex-husbands you've got but we're coming up on some pretty big gators up ahead, in case any of them look familiar.

CELESTE

Just the one ex-husband and he lasted less than a year.

BREE

It was kind of like a false start marriage, so she had to go back to the starting line.

CATHERINE

I don't see anything.

CELESTE

Oh, I see! I see their beady little eyes sticking up out of the water. If I had any more ex-husbands besides Earl, I'm sure there would be a resemblance.

REGINA

I'm just curious, Thibaut. When did you think getting out in a boat among all these prehistoric looking monsters was a good thing?

THIBAUT

I've been doing this my entire life. I was raised in a cabin on Barataria Bayou in Jefferson Parish.

CATHERINE

So, you're a real Cajun?

THIBAUT

My daddy was a full-blooded Cajun, descended straight from the Acadians.

BREE

The Acadians?

THIBAUT

The French who settled Novia Scotia, but were run out when the Brits took over. Cajun, I guess, is a lazy way to say Acadian.

CELESTE

So, Cajuns are French Canadians who got run off into the wilds of Louisiana?

THIBAUT

That's right. Some of the Cajuns that live out in the swamps still speak only French.

MARY GRACE

What about Creole?

REGINA

Yeah Thibaut, do you have any Creole in your blood?

THIBAUT

I've got a dash of Creole. My mother descended from Spanish and Haitian lines.

REGINA

A dash of Creole, huh? So, I guess that makes you a spicy Cajun. Yum Yum.

CELESTE/BREE/MARY GRACE/CATHERINE

Regina!

REGINA

I'm just saying's all!

THIBAUT

That's OK, Regina. My Momma was a fiery woman. Taught me everything I knew about hunting and trapping.

CELESTE

Your MOMMA taught you those things?

THIBAUT

Yes, she did. She used to shoot rabbits, muskrat, and possum.

REGINA

And you ate it?

THIBAUT

I sure did. My father would be out for a month at a time crabbing, fishing, or shrimping. We had to eat while he was gone.

MARY GRACE

You're a real survivalist. You could actually live off the land if you had to.

THIBAUT

Most people who were raised in the bayou can. My Mom made extra money by trapping river rats for fur coats. She made a pretty penny before the anti-fur freaks took over.

CATHERINE

A fur coat made out of river rat?

THIBAUT

The proper name is nutria but around here it's known as river rat or swamp rat. They're interchangeable.

CELESTE

Now listen here.

BREE
Heel Celeste.
CELESTE
I don't know how you could justify murdering a
sweet harmless little creature just so people
can stay warm.
THIBAUT
Celeste, is it? Have you ever been really
cold? Somehow, I doubt it. Nutria are
considered a "guilt free" fur, socially
acceptable and environmentally friendly.
CELESTE
You expect me to believe that?
REGINA
Oo, I wish I had some popcorn.
THIBAUT
I don't really care if you believe it or not.
BREE
Oh no.
THIBAUT
Nutrias destroy the ecosystem and kill the
vegetation hundreds of other creatures depend
on. They aren't native to Louisiana. They're
an invasive species.
REGINA
Damn it! This calls for popcorn.
THIBAUT
They live a cage free life unlike other
animals raised for their fur and they're
better for the environment than petroleum
based fake fur. Plus you can eat them.
CELESTE
No one will ever accept it.
THIBAUT
Really? Because in the past few years Michael
Kors and Oscar de la Renta have been using
them for fur trims. Greta Garbo's favorite fur
was Nutria back in the day.

CATHERINE
(Catherine points.)
An alligator!
MARY GRACE
Saved by the alligator. How ironic.
THIBAUT
That's Beauregard. He's the biggest gator in
this bayou. As a matter of fact I've got a
surprise for y'all.

THIBAUT reaches into his backpack.

CATHERINE
Please don't throw Celeste in. I know she can
be overbearing but she IS our friend.

THIBAUT pulls out a plastic alligator.

THIBAUT
This is one of Beauregard's babies. She got
orphaned when someone killed her Momma for her
meat and didn't realize she had babies. Each
of us guides took a baby to foster. This is
Evangeline. When she's big enough, I'll
release her back in the bayou with her daddy.
I just hope Beauregard doesn't eat her.
REGINA
See Celeste. You think the humans are always
the bad guys.
THIBAUT
Baby alligators only have a 3 to 4 percent
survival rate.
MARY GRACE
This is like a real Trials of Life video.
CELESTE
I guess you guys are right. Nature can be a
bitch.
REGINA
Maybe you should apologize to Thibaut. For

heaven's sake, the man is a surrogate mother to an alligator. That takes someone pretty special.

THIBAUT

Well, thank you ma'am.

CELESTE

I'm sorry.

THIBAUT

Apology accepted.

BREE

Let me see that baby. I got to hold a baby alligator when I was on a commercial for the Mississippi State Zoo.

CATHERINE

How'd you get that gig?

BREE

I went on to win Miss Waffle Barn Mississippi. Weirdly after I won Miss Waffle Barn Interstate 55 Exit 29A, my biggest competitor at the state pageant was the Queen right across the bridge, Miss Waffle Barn Interstate 55 Exit 29B. But unfortunately, there was an "incident," and I won the state crown.

CATHERINE

The "incident" didn't have anything to do with a baton or a karate chop, did it?

BREE

(Whispering to the baby alligator.) We'll never tell. Will we, Evangaline?

THIBAUT

Now on to see the wild boars!

REGINA

Oh no!

INTERMISSION

ACT TWO
Scene 1

The flat. There is a sign that reads Ball
Gowns by Blaise. BLAISE enters, holding a
clipboard. He is dressed to the nines. He
brushes off the shoulders of his suit with his
palm and straightens his suit jacket.

BLAISE
(Addressing an invisible cameraman out toward
the audience)
Yes. The camera should go right there... A
little to the left...No! No! My left, your
right. *(There's a pause)*
You need to do a sound test? Hmmm. Testing.
123. *(another pause)* Tell a joke? Let me
think... *(clears throat)* Oh, OK I've got one.
What happens when you sing country music
backwards? You get your wife and your job
back. How do you know if you are trailer park
trash? Your house moves but your twelve cars
don't! You know you're a redneck if you think
a Nutcracker is jumping off the high dive. Oh
honey, I could do this all night.
(Pause) Oh, we're good now?

CELESTE enters in a beautiful ball gown.

CELESTE
Oh Blaise! I haven't had time to thank you for
letting us use this gorgeous apartment. And to
think it's right on Bourbon Street!
BLAISE
It's vacant for the next two weeks. It belongs
to my friends, Troy and Rodney. They got into
a little lover's spat so Rodney took Troy on a

cruise to the French Riviera to make it up to him.

CELESTE
Earl used to think that putting his own supper plate in the dishwasher or picking his underwear up off the floor was good enough to make up with me. And you're telling me Mr. Troy got a cruise? Maybe I'm playing for the wrong team.

BLAISE
Or maybe you just haven't found the right person. I know a good man is hard to find, but I bet he's out there.

BLAISE/CELESTE
(Cross their fingers)
Let's hope!

CELESTE
Are you ready to get started?

BLAISE
Absolutely! I noticed you've gotten thirty thousand more followers since you called me.

CELESTE
I must admit the web series really is taking off. I've been contacted for a possible pilot!

BLAISE
Pilots are the best! Both kinds!

Celeste looks out at the imaginary camera man.

CELESTE
Ready?... O.K. Blaise you stand here. Ready girls?!

ALL
(O.S.)
Yes!

REGINA
(O.S.)
Ready as I'll ever be!

CELESTE

(Looks out at the "camera man")

3..2..1..Hello! And welcome to another episode
of Say Yes to Anything But a Wedding Dress.
That's right. Say yes to any other type of
dress that can make you happy when you slip it
over your head without the commitment of a
wedding dress. Anything but a dress that
symbolizes the binding of your body, mind,
soul, and bank account to a man who might turn
out to be not your soul mate but a person that
you actually despise waking up to day after
day after day..

REGINA

(O.S.)

They get it Celeste. You hated Earl. Move on!

CELESTE

Today we're in The Big Easy. That's right. New
Orleans. I'd like to welcome our guest, Blaise
Benoit, owner of Ball Gowns by Blaise, located
right here in the French Quarter on Royal
Street. Welcome to Say Yes to Anything But a
Wedding Dress, Blaise.

BLAISE

I'm thrilled to be here, Celeste... with you
and your friends who, by the way America, are
not models, but FRIENDS you've brought with
you from Flovilla, Alabama.
Welcome to New Orleans!

CELESTE

That's right y'all. My friends and I have come
to the great crescent city to experience Mardi
Gras up close and personal. While here, we'll
be attending one of the most famous Mardi Gras
Balls, the Bacchus Ball.

BLAISE

Celeste, these balls have been a traditional
Mardi Gras event since Louisiana was just a
French colony.

CELESTE
Blaise, what are some of the challenges of designing gowns for one of these traditional balls?

BLAISE
I'd say the most important thing is the fabric. These balls can be extremely sweaty. All the dancing and merry making and extreme humidity make for some very hot and steamy balls.

CELESTE
Anything else?

BLAISE
Yes, since thē balls are BYOB I try not to design gowns with trains since the guest will possibly be dragging a cooler behind her.

REGINA
(O.S.)
BYOB?! Hallelujah! That's gonna save us a bundle!

CELESTE
We are ROLLING REGINA!

REGINA
(O.S.)
Sorry!

CELESTE
You were saying?

BLAISE
One fun thing about the balls is that the floats actually come straight from the parade route right into the convention center. One year a float driver was so drunk he took out a few revelers but the party kept going. As the French say, c'est la vie!

CELESTE
Oh my! Could you explain the tradition of the mask that is worn by Mardi Gras participants?

BLAISE

Oh yes. The tradition of the mask goes back
ages. You see, everyone wanted to get all the
partying and sin out of their system before
they had to commit to Lent, which is basically
giving up anything enjoyable for forty days.
Thank the good Lord I'm not Catholic. As I
was saying people wanted to get all of the
naughtiness out of their system so they'd go
bat shit crazy, oh wait...can I say that on
air?

CELESTE

We can edit that out.

BLAISE

Celeste, before the forty days of Lent, these
people go nuttier than a squirrel turd. (*to
Celeste*) Is that better?

CELESTE

Maybe.

BLAISE

These people go hog wild! So, they wear masks
so nobody will know who they are when they're
engaging in all these wild antics before the
clock strikes midnight on Fat Tuesday and
they're back to being good Catholics.
Oh, the debauchery! Drinking, dancing, nudity!

CELESTE

Nudity?!

BLAISE

Oh yes. Some people say that Christmas is the
most wonderful time of the year, but if you
live in New Orleans, you know that's not true.
It's Mardi Gras, honey!

CELESTE

People actually get naked?

BLAISE

You wouldn't believe what some of these folks
will do for a one cent string of plastic beads

from China. Some of them get naked as a boiled
chicken.

REGINA
(O.S.)
I'm writing this whole trip off as research
for my one nine hundred number! This just
keeps getting better and better!

CELESTE
Regina!

REGINA
(O.S.)
Sorry!

CELESTE
Without further ado. We'd like to show off our
lovely ball gowns to the viewers. First, we
have Regina.

REGINA enters.

REGINA
It is about time. I have an appointment with a
hurricane at Pat O'Brien's.

BLAISE
Ladies and gentlemen, appropriately enough
Regina is wearing a sequined gown, guaranteed
to disguise the spill of any drink at the ball
whether it be a hurricane, Vieux Carré
Cocktail, or a Sazerac.

REGINA
Or in my case, possibly all three. I've got to
make up for lost time.

CELESTE
Lost time?

REGINA
I've been in New Orleans almost twenty-four
hours and I've yet to go to Pat O'Brien's
piano bar, have a drink, and dance on a table,
possibly topless, I haven't decided yet.

Blaise shoves Regina away.

BLAISE
Oh my! NEXT, we have Bree in an elegant gold gown.

BREE enters in a tight gold dress.

BREE
I look like the Oscar statue with boobs.
CELESTE
Tell us about the color choice, Blaise.
BLAISE
Gold is one of the traditional Mardi Gras colors symbolizing power. The other two Mardi Gras colors are green and purple.
BREE
What do green and purple represent?
BLAISE
Purple symbolizes justice and Green symbolizes faith. In the past if parade attendees exhibited these traits, they would get tokens or beads tossed to them. For example, if you saw one of your loyal, faithful friends along the parade route you might throw him a strand of green beads symbolizing his faithfulness.
CELESTE
Well, I can tell you who I wouldn't be throwing green beads to.
BLAISE
I'm going to go out on a limb here and guess, Earl?
CELESTE
You're darn tootin'. He was about as faithful as a wild rabbit.
BLAISE
(Pushing Bree away)
Next!

CATHERINE enters in a purple dress.

CELESTE
Our next guest on Say Yes to Anything But a Wedding Dress is Catherine, who is wearing a lovely purple gown.

BLAISE
Catherine is wearing a Vincent Vanderpool ball gown in Mardi Gras purple. In the past the color purple was reserved for royalty.

CATHERINE
Oo. Since I'm wearing purple I'm kind of like the Queen Bee. I love it.

REGINA
I wouldn't get too excited about that. You know if the Queen Bee doesn't live up to the expectations of the hive, the drones gang up on her and sting her to death. Then they have her replaced.

CELESTE
Regina, we are rolling! I'm going to have to edit out all this extra commentary.

REGINA
Fine. But one last thing, Barney is purple too but everybody hates him.

CELESTE
Regina!

REGINA
I'm kidding! I promise I'll be good.

MARY GRACE enters.

BLAISE
Next, we have Mary Grace wearing a beautiful Jester inspired gown perfect for a Mardi Gras Ball.

REGINA
Watch out world. Ronald McDonald's got some competition.

BLAISE

The jester is a popular symbol for Mardi Gras. Traditionally the jester character entertains everyone by pointing out weaknesses in others.

MARY GRACE

Pointing out weaknesses in others? We have a symbol for that too in Alabama. It's called a Lillian, otherwise known as my mother-in-law.

(All the ladies are in a line.)

CELESTE

So, everyone, there you have it. Ball gowns that we'll be wearing to the Bacchus Mardi Gras Ball, courtesy of Ball Gowns by Blaise on Royal Street right here in the heart of the French Quarter in New Orleans. Join us next time on Say Yes to Anything But a Wedding Dress when we'll be choosing the perfect funeral dress. Not a standard black dress to wear to a funeral, but we'll be choosing the actual dresses we'd like to spend eternity in.

MARY GRACE

What?!

CELESTE

That's right Mary Grace. Why trust your husband, one of your children, or heaven forbid your mother-in-law to pick out the dress you'll literally be wearing for an eternity? Join us next week on Say Yes to Anything But a Wedding Dress when we'll be picking out that funeral dress, the most important dress of your life...well, of your death.

(The ladies stare at Celeste in disbelief. Celeste looks out at the "cameraman".)

CELESTE
Thank you, Darryl! That's a wrap!

ACT TWO
Scene 2

The ladies enter the Bacchus Ball. This can be staged with just party atmosphere lighting, background music, and a round table. Celeste is dragging a small cooler.

CELESTE
Ladies, we can now check off attending a Mardi Gras Ball from the bucket list.
BREE
This is quite the shindig.
MARY GRACE
I'd better not be the only woman here with a ball gown inspired by a clown.
CELESTE
It's not a clown. It's a jester.
CATHERINE
In the English courts he was known as a licensed fool.
MARY GRACE
Thanks Catherine.
CATHERINE
I honestly think that this is the only time my class in Medieval Studies ever came in handy.
MARY GRACE
Why did an accounting major take medieval studies?
CATHERINE
Why do any freshman girls take any of their classes? Because the professor was smoking hot.
REGINA
Catherine! Rrrr! *(Growls and paws like a cougar.)* We've got a live one ladies!
I have news for y'all. I'm not going to be doing a lot of sitting. I'm going to be getting my groove on.

CATHERINE
You know, Regina, I'm going out there with
you. Thinking about being young again chasing
after hot professors makes me want to get my
groove back.
REGINA
Let's go! You guys pour us a drink from the
cooler of happiness. We'll be back in a few.

REGINA and CATHERINE dance off.

CELESTE
It's a good thing Blaise told us the ball
wasn't only BYOB but it was BYO Food. I'm
famished.
MARY GRACE
I have to visit the ladies' room before the
line gets too long.
BREE
It sucks getting old. Instead of thinking
about dancing and drinking and getting all of
our naughtiness out of us before Lent, we have
to concentrate on prophylactic bathroom breaks
before the lines become unbearable and
one of us has a situation worthy of an
incontinence undergarment commercial. Did you
know they come in THONGS now?
MARY GRACE
Would you wear one of those?
BREE
It depends.
CELESTE
Y'all go on. I'll unpack our food and start
making drinks for everybody.

*BREE and MARY GRACE exit. CELESTE begins
unpacking the subs, glasses, etc. THIBAUT
enters wearing a tux with tails and holding a
cocktail.*

THIBAUT
That's a lot of food for one person. And I
hope you're not planning on drinking all of
that tonight.
CELESTE
The night is still young, but nah, I'm just
setting the table. Half my party is on the
dance floor and half are in the ladies' room.
THIBAUT
And you're playing hostess at The Bacchus
Ball.
CELESTE
Looks that way. You taking a break from the
swamp? I must say you clean up rather nicely.
THIBAUT
Well, thank you. I'm heading over to have my
fortune told.
CELESTE
Who's going to tell it?
THIBAUT
See that little tent set up over there that
says VooDoo Priestess?
CELESTE
Surely don't believe that stuff, do you?
THIBAUT
The Bacchus Krewe just provides fun little
diversions at the ball like VooDoo Priestesses
because I guess you can't really just dance
all night.
CELESTE
From the looks of it I think Regina and
Catherine might disagree.
THIBAUT
Maybe save me a dance for later?
CELESTE
Oh, absolutely. Maybe you can tell me what the
voodoo priestess sees in your future or maybe
you could just sit by me and I could make up

some mumbo jumbo and save you the trip to the
VooDoo Temple Tent.
THIBAUT
Maybe you should let her read your fortune.
Could be good news coming your way. You never
know. Anyway, like I said, it's just a fun
activity we usually do at the ball.
CELESTE
You've been to this before?
THIBAUT
I was born into the Krewe as they say. My
mother was a third generation Krewe member.
CELESTE
That's interesting. I guess the most similar
thing I'm familiar with is when your mother
might have been a Tri Delta so you have legacy
status, but being born into something is kind
of like royalty.
THIBAUT
As a matter of fact, they'll be announcing the
King and Queen of the Ball at the end of the
night, so I guess you're kind of right.
CELESTE
You've got to be kidding. Sounds like a
glorified prom.
THIBAUT
Some might think so if they didn't know the
whole story. The King and the Queen are the
two folks who throw this shindig. Each year
they raise all the money and plan the whole
thing. Their identity remains a mystery for an
entire year until the night of the ball.
Some folks think they kind of earn the title.
CELESTE
O.K. I take back what I said. I had to plan a
bridesmaid's luncheon for my niece once who
was a true bridezilla from Hell and I almost
had to be committed, so Hail to the King and

Queen! I can't imagine being responsible for something this grand.

THIBAUT

See you later?

CELESTE

I'll fuel up with a hurricane and be raring to go.

THIBAUT

Sounds good.

CELESTE

I hope you get a fortunate fortune.

THIBAUT heads to the VooDoo Priestess tent. MARY GRACE and BREE enter.

CELESTE

Can you believe the guy from the swamp tour is here?

MARY GRACE

Heavens to Betsy, Celeste. I'm sure he doesn't spend all his time in the swamp. He is a business owner after all.

BREE

And he's fostering a baby alligator. It takes someone special to take that on.

CELESTE

He was heading over to that VooDoo Priestess tent to get his fortune told. Don't y'all think that's weird?

BREE

Here are a few things that seem weird. God sent John the book of Revelation from a crack in the top of a cave. Most hotels do not have a thirteenth floor. We were told for years that Pluto was a planet and suddenly we're supposed to believe it's not.

MARY GRACE

Bree's got a point, Celeste. We can't be poo pooing what other people might or might not

believe. I mean, I don't care that the Book of Revelation came from a crack in a cave. When Pastor Brown talks about the four horsemen of the apocalypse, I check the status of my relationship with my maker... You know, come to think of it, I want MY fortune read.
BREE
What about Leviticus 19:26 - You shall not interpret omens or tell fortunes.
MARY GRACE
I'm not the one doing the telling. I'm just gonna be the one doing the listening.

BREE and MARY GRACE head to VooDoo Priestess tent. REGINA and CATHERINE enter.

CELESTE
The dancing queens have returned.
REGINA
Not for long. I just requested the Cha Cha Slide.
CATHERINE
And I requested the Macarena.
CELESTE
What has gotten into you two?
REGINA
I don't know if you've noticed Celeste, but we're not exactly getting any younger.
CATHERINE
Exactly! I got to thinking, what if this is the last dance I ever go to? It's not like Flovilla, Alabama is teaming with dancing opportunities. I want to know if it turns out to be my last time ever dancing that I maxed it out.
REGINA
I'm telling you, removing that ascot got Catherine's blood pumping again. That thing

was acting as a fun tourniquet. I swear! Now look at her, dancing the night away. Fun's just oozing all through her body now.

CATHERINE

What about you, Celeste? You've played ball hostess long enough. You put out the food and drink and now it's time for you to get on that dance floor.

CELESTE

I promise I will. Just let me finish my pub sub and get a little liquid courage coursing through my veins.

REGINA

Since when did you need liquid courage?

CELESTE

Since Mr. Cajun Critters Swamp Tour Man asked me for a dance after he had his fortune read by some VooDoo Priestess.

REGINA

He's here?!

CATHERINE

Only in New Orleans can you have Swamp Critters and VooDoo Priestesses occur in the same sentence! A Toast!

REGINA/CATHERINE

To the Big Easy!

REGINA

Come on! We can eat when we're dead. I don't want to miss the Cha Cha Slide!

CATHERINE

Let's Carpe this damn Diem!

REGINA

Yes! Before we kick the bucket. One more toast. To no more fun tourniquets!

CATHERINE

Here! Here!

REGINA and CATHERINE exit.

CELESTE
There go the dancing queens and here I sit all
by myself like a nervous little school girl
waiting on Thibaut to get his fortune read.
Hmmm. I wonder if Miss VooDoo Priestess told
him anything about me? What am I thinking?
This woman is a hired hand to entertain drunk
ball attendees.

MARY GRACE and BREE enter.

MARY GRACE
I did it. I was told my fortune by the VooDoo
Priestess Madam Marie... Oh Lord please don't
damn me to Hell.
CELESTE
And?
BREE
It's good news!
CELESTE
I would imagine it would be. I'm sure the
Bacchus Ball folks who hired her wouldn't want
her pissing everybody off with a bad fortune.
MARY GRACE
She said when I walked in the tent, that there
was an aura of green all around me, so she
thinks I might come into some money soon.
CELESTE
What if it means you're green with envy about
something.
MARY GRACE
It can't mean that. I'm very content with my
life. I can't stand Lillian but I'm not
jealous of her.
BREE
It's true Celeste. I'd bet Mary Grace is the
most content friend we have despite her
dealings with her monster in law.

CELESTE

Mary Grace, you know in cartoons when they surround a person with a green haze? It's usually trying to convey that they smell bad. Did you have onions on your salad at lunch?

MARY GRACE

Well, IF I smell bad, I would hope my friends would tell me and not let me walk around stinking up the place. I'm just gonna go with what the VooDoo Priestess said and assume I will have a windfall of some sort. Maybe Lillian will kick the bucket soon. Who knows?

CELESTE

Mary Grace! That's terrible.

MARY GRACE

I know. I've got two strikes tonight. I consulted a soothsayer and took pleasure in the thought of my mean mother-in-law dying. New Orleans has turned me into a complete heathen.

BREE

I guess they don't call it Sin City for nothing.

CELESTE

I'm going to see the VooDoo Priestess. Lord, please forgive me because I'm about to sin.

MARY GRACE

You know I don't think you can get forgiveness if you go in knowing you're sinning.

BREE

Lighten up Mary Grace! Neither one of us is going to be casting the first stone. You just broke some Old Testament law knowingly and I'm about to sit down here and knowingly drink a Hurricane. Go see the VooDoo Priestess with our blessing, Celeste.

MARY GRACE

Speak for yourself Bree. Sorry Celeste, I

can't give it my blessing but you better tell
me everything she says!

ACT TWO
Scene 3

VOODOO PRIESTESS is sitting at a draped table.
CELESTE cautiously approaches.

VOODOO PRIESTESS
Come in, Come in. Ah, what was it you said. It
was strange going to a VooDoo Priestess? No,
no, that wasn't the word. What was it... Weird.
Yes, weird.
CELESTE
You must have little microphones at all the
tables or something.
VOODOO PRIESTESS
Hmmm. How would I know your voice? There are
hundreds of people at the ball.
CELESTE
True. But-
VOODOO PRIESTESS
A non-believer. That's fine. But if you don't
believe, why are you here?
CELESTE
I'm not sure. I guess to hear my fortune. And
at least don't tell me I'm about to come into
money.
VOODOO PRIESTESS
Oh, you must be friends with the green girl.
You wait and see. Maybe she'll give you a
loan.
CELESTE
I don't need a loan.
VOODOO PRIESTESS
That's good because there's no green at all
around you. Just so you know.
CELESTE
Can we get started?

VOODOO PRIESTESS
Of course.

The PRIESTESS closes her eyes and tosses some small bones onto the table. She studies the bones. Her eyes become wide.

CELESTE
What are those?
VOODOO PRIESTESS
Possum bones.
CELESTE
Ewe.
VOODOO PRIESTESS
Possums speak with the spirits at night.
CELESTE
Ah huh.
VOODOO PRIESTESS
You say you don't believe in VooDoo, correct?
CELESTE
I guess. I mean. No, I don't believe. I think you were hired as more of an entertainer.
VOODOO PRIESTESS
That's good.
CELESTE
Why is that good? What do you see?
VOODOO PRIESTESS
The bones tell me that Celeste Abercrombie Scarborough will soon cease to exist.

ACT TWO
Scene 4

*The flat. MARY GRACE, BREE, REGINA and
CATHERINE are having coffee.*

MARY GRACE
Don't y'all think one of us should go in there
to at least see if Celeste is still breathing?
REGINA
It's not going to be me. If she has ceased
breathing, I'm gonna freak out. I do a lot of
things, but I don't do dead.
BREE
Regina! That is a terrible way to talk about
your friend!
REGINA
If she's no longer with us then she's not
really a friend anymore, now is she?
MARY GRACE
I can't believe you.
REGINA
I don't know what's so hard to believe. I
don't want to be in a room alone with a dead
body whether they're my friend or not.
CATHERINE
How in the world do you ever go to a funeral?
REGINA
I don't.
BREE
You cannot tell me you've never been to a
funeral.
REGINA
I can and I will tell you that. I always come
down with a terrible case of funeral flu.
Mother did the prepayment and preplanning of
her celebration of life service and that's
exactly what I did. I celebrated the fact that

she had herself and daddy cremated so I didn't
have to come down with the funeral flu.
CATHERINE
Why does this not shock me?

CELESTE enters in an Indian tunic.

BREE
Are you O.K.? We wondered if you'd died in
your sleep in there you've been in bed so
long.
CELESTE
Let's see Bree. It might be that I'm just a
little depressed that a VooDoo Priestess
thinks that I'm not going to "exist much
longer."
BREE
One day you are going to cease to exist
Celeste, but I don't think it's going to be
any time soon. You're being ridiculous.
CELESTE
She KNEW things, Bree! Things that she
couldn't possibly know.
CATHERINE
Maybe it's a ploy to get you to visit her and
pay for a better fortune telling experience.
CELESTE
I don't think so. She didn't give me a card or
any indication where she could be found for me
to inquire further about my predicted demise.
As a matter of fact, she calmly told me that
she was going to the bar for her second
complimentary glass of wine that evening,
and after that she was headed to the dance
floor, that she had read all the fortunes she
intended to for the night.
MARY GRACE
That is weird.

REGINA

Can we continue this VooDoo talk over lunch please? Do y'all know how long I've waited to have a famous turducken from K-Paul's Kitchen? I'm not leaving the French Quarter until we eat at K-Paul's and I figure today is as good a day as any.

BREE

What in Heaven's name is a turducken, may I ask?

REGINA

It's when they stuff a chicken into a duck then stuff the duck into a turkey. Like an edible birdfest.

BREE

Well count me in. At least we know we won't walk out of there hungry, which is more than I can say for any French place. I refuse to go to a French restaurant anymore, ever since Ronnie and I went to Chez Marcel and I had to order three entrees to have a complete meal.

REGINA

Y'all might as well get ready because I plan on deviling myself today so I'll probably need a recovery nap later.

CATHERINE

I just don't understand when you say you're gonna devil yourself. You mean like deviling an egg? Stuffing it with something?

MARY GRACE

Actually to devil something in culinary circles means to make it zesty, although southern deviled eggs are pretty tame in the spice category.

BREE

I'll say. That little bit of mustard is hardly zesty and does paprika even have a taste?

CELESTE
That's a good point. It's really just a dusty
food coloring if you ask me.
CATHERINE
Can we get back to my original question about
deviling yourself?
CELESTE
How do you not know about the deviling
incident?
BREE
Catherine didn't move over to Flovilla until
after the incident.
CELESTE
That's right. A transplant from Fort Payne.
Practically a foreigner. Regina, since the
incident happened at your house you should do
the honors.
REGINA
Magnolia Oaks Subdivision hosted an amateur
barbecue contest before the Pig Jig started.
It was called Praise the Lard. Later we had to
change the name because the Pentecostals on
the cul de sac got all bent out of shape. So
Praise the Lard became The Magnolia Oaks Holy
Smokes Contest. They complained a little
after that but we just ignored them.
BREE
Can we get to the deviling?
REGINA
ANYWAY, my Richard and some of his golfing
buddies decided to enter the competition.
Richard's friend Bobby Lively proceeded to
trim all the excess fat off the cuts of meat,
not realizing that our bull dog, Devil, had
parked himself directly under the table from
where all this fat was falling like dog manna
from heaven. Unfortunately, like a hungry
scooter ridin' redneck at an all you can eat

buffet, Devil downed every last bit of that leftover fat.

CATHERINE

Uh oh.

REGINA

Uh oh is right. Later that night, Devil died under that same table, lying on his back with head cocked, legs up and mouth open. No one knew if he died in that position lying in wait for more fat to fall from the sky or if he just kind of keeled over like a dying cockroach.

MARY GRACE

Regina swore he died with a smile on his face, but we were pretty sure it was just his under bite showing from his jowls being pulled back by gravity.

BREE

After Devil's tragic demise, anyone who would eat to the point of discomfort would say something like "I'm just deviling myself with this second helping of macaroni and cheese," or we'd say, "Don't devil yourself with all that coca cola cake."

REGINA

So, the logical next question is - Celeste, are you wearing that getup to lunch?

ACT TWO
Scene 5

REGINA, MARY GRACE, BREE, CATHERINE, and CELESTE are center, "walking" to K-Paul's Kitchen.

REGINA
According to my GPS we walk five blocks down Bourbon and take a left on...SHAR TRAY Street.
BREE
That's Sharht in French.
REGINA
But we're not in France.
MARY GRACE
Luckily there is nothing that Google can't answer. *(She pokes around on her phone.)* New Orleans natives pronounce it CHARTERS street.
REGINA
Charters? Well, that's no fun. Shar Tray it is.
CELESTE
Look! A parade is coming this way!
BREE
I thought all the Mardi Gras Parades were only at night.
CELESTE
Apparently not.
CATHERINE
I have an idea.
REGINA
I have an idea too. Let's get moving and beat this parade down the street so I can get to my turducken.
CATHERINE
It's like you said Regina. The fun tourniquet is off and my idea is that we join in this parade.

MARY GRACE
I don't even know if that's legal.

CATHERINE
Well I've certainly never heard of anybody being arrested for joining in a Mardi Gras parade.

CELESTE
Exactly how many Mardi Gras parades have you been to?

CATHERINE
All right, but still. We can check it off the bucket list.

MARY GRACE
Last time I checked, marching in a Mardi Gras parade wasn't on the bucket list.

CATHERINE
Well pencil it in because I'm going to do it.

CELESTE
(to Regina)
I blame you for this. You made her take off the ascot.

CATHERINE
It was a scarf!

REGINA
Au contraire. It was a fun tourniquet. I'm sorry Celeste! I didn't know she was going to bleed out!

CATHERINE
Here they come! Let's do this!

The actor playing BLAISE dances across the stage in a Carnivale type costume showing some skin. The ladies join in doing some spontaneous moves. The actor dances off with a flourish. CATHERINE turns her back to the audience and flips up her shirt.

MARY GRACE
Catherine! Stop that! What's gotten into you?!

CATHERINE flips down her shirt and turns around toward Mary Grace.

CATHERINE
Don't have a hemorrhage, Mary Grace. I have on a bra.
REGINA
I don't!

REGINA turns with her back to the audience and flips up her shirt.

REGINA
WOOOOOOO HOOOOOO!

Someone tosses some beads toward REGINA from the wings.

CELESTE
Stop that! What are you thinking? We need to go eat and I've got to come up with a solution to my situation!
BREE
Ah ladies, I think we might have a more pressing situation at the moment. This is the Krewe of Yuga. It's apparently the Homosexual Mardi Gras Krewe.
MARY GRACE
How do you know?
BREE
Because that float behind us is made of rainbows and says "It's Raining Men."
REGINA
We're marching in a pride parade?!
CATHERINE
Oh my God. Are those guys dressed up like the village people?!!

MARY GRACE
IS THAT A CNN CAMERA???!!!
Parade Participant dances back across the stage to "It's Raining Men" as the ladies disperse frantically.

ACT TWO
Scene 6

The flat. CELESTE, REGINA, MARY GRACE,
CATHERINE, and BREE are lounging around in a
state of lethargy after the turducken meal.
MARY GRACE is holding a small book.

BREE
I'm in a food coma.
REGINA
It's great, isn't it?
CELESTE
Do you have any idea how many hours of yoga
I'll have to do to combat the effects of the
turducken?
REGINA
I have no idea, but I know how many I'll have
to do.
CELESTE
How many?
REGINA
None. Because I don't care.
MARY GRACE
I'm glad somebody doesn't care. I'm sitting
over here wondering how my mother's going to
react when she sees me dancing around with a
bunch of other women in a gay pride parade.
CATHERINE
It wasn't really a gay pride parade it was a
Mardi Gras parade being put on by a gay Krewe.
CELESTE
They looked pretty proud if you ask me. That
Village People Cowboy in the assless chaps had
a better butt than I'll ever have no matter
how much yoga I do. Not that it matters since
I'll be dead soon. (*Weepily*) I've taken such
good care of myself for nothing.

REGINA

Now aren't you happy you stopped that foolish
vegetarian thing and ate some turducken today?
At least if you do drop dead, you'll do it
with a full stomach.

MARY GRACE

(*Looking at her phone*)

Oh, my Lord. The gay Krewe of Yuga's nick name
is KY!

REGINA

(*Starts laughing so hard she falls off
the couch/chair*)

MARY GRACE

I'm glad you think this is funny, Regina. My
mother is head of the social committee at
Flovilla Baptist. She liked to have gone to be
home with the Lord when I married Kenneth and
became a Methodist. I am not invited to any
more social functions with the Baptists
as it is. Now she's gonna see me on CNN and
think I'm in Sin City living my true
life...(*whispers loudly*) "as a lesbian." Not
that there's anything wrong with that.
It's just that, I'm not.

CATHERINE

I'm thinking your mother is more of a Fox News
gal.

MARY GRACE

But she gets bored during the commercials and
flips to CNN, Catherine!

BREE

I hate to point this out but you just thought
you had a problem with your mother-in-law
before. If she sees you in the homosexual
Mardi Gras parade, there's no telling what
she'll try to do.

CELESTE

Yeah, she'll probably demand that Kenneth

leave you, or she'll cut y'all out of the will.

MARY GRACE
P-lease! Kenneth is like every other red-blooded man, if he thought I'd turned to ladies he'd probably just follow me around like a puppy dog hoping to get in on the action.

REGINA
Mary Grace! We may have to put Catherine's fun tourniquet on you if you keep it up!....Nah, that wouldn't be any fun.

CATHERINE
Celeste, I guess it's a good thing you won't be around to hear the gossip of how we all came out of the closet at Mardi Gras.

CELESTE
Not funny, Catherine. I'm going to figure out how to break this curse or whatever's going on here.

CELESTE exits.

MARY GRACE
I'm gonna read some more of my new book to get my mind off the parade fiasco.

REGINA
What did you end up getting at that souvenir shop, Mary Grace?

MARY GRACE
A brief history of New Orleans. It's fascinating so far. Apparently, our building was one of MANY houses of ill repute. New Orleans was a favorite port of call for sailors. They had these guide books called Pleasure Guides. It listed prostitutes with their pictures and *(She looks at the book)* meticulously described the sexual specialties and background of each one.

CATHERINE
Talk about TMI!
MARY GRACE
(Reading from book) Here's an example. Miss Delphine Delizy. She is thirty-eight, but we are duty bound to state that she is still of very appetizing aspect .... and there is nothing in the whole catalogue of Cupid's diversions that she has not done.
REGINA
Cupid's diversions? Really?
MARY GRACE
And there's Leonide Leblanc. It is difficult to do justice to such a celebrated woman ... she has charmed a generation and every notable rake has passed at least one night in her arms.
BREE
It's like these prostitutes are celebrated. Reminds me of the Kardashians.
MARY GRACE
Y'all remember when I googled this address and it said it had been home to not only a convent but also that pirate and a voodoo priestess?
CATHERINE/BREE/REGINA
Yeah, yes, etc.
MARY GRACE
It wasn't just any old voodoo priestess. It was the most famous voodoo priestess, Marie Leveau.
CATHERINE
That was the name of that voodoo shop Celeste made us stop at. Marie Laveau's House of VooDoo.
REGINA
Yeah, with all those scary masks and voodoo dolls.
BREE
And incense and herbs and stuff. That place

was stinking so bad I had to walk out of
there. It was ruining the taste of my
hurricane.
REGINA
Good thing you can drink on the street here.
Flovilla needs to take note.
BREE
Good luck with that.

CELESTE enters and listens.

MARY GRACE
Back to the voodoo priestess. Marie Laveau was
called The VooDoo Queen and she lived in this
building.
CELESTE
What was that?
MARY GRACE
Nothing. *(She slams the book closed.)*
CELESTE
Marie Laveau lived right here?
MARY GRACE
Maybe, but it doesn't mean a thing.
There is a knock on the door. CELESTE answers.

*MARIE, a maid, stands in the doorway. She's
wearing a dull gray maid's dress with apron.*

MARIE
Hi, I'm from Merry Maids. Blaise sent me over
to clean the apartment for y'all.
CELESTE
We didn't ask for that.
REGINA
Well don't be questioning it. Let the woman
in.
MARIE
It's a courtesy, he said. He said something
about getting a lot of dress orders.

CELESTE
What's your name?
MARIE
(MARIE points to her name tag.) Marie?
CELESTE
Come in. *(to the ladies)* This is a sign!
REGINA
No, I think it's like she said. It's not a
sign, it's just a courtesy.
CATHERINE
She's a maid, Celeste.
CELESTE
(accusingly) ARE you?
MARIE
Yes.
CELESTE
Let me ask. Do you happen to practice VooDoo?
MARIE
No, I'm a Catholic.
CELESTE
Close enough!

*Celeste drags Marie over to a chair and sits
her down.*

MARIE
What?!
CELESTE
I've been reading up on how to break this hex
or curse or whatever is wrong with me. And I
believe you've been sent to help.
MARIE
I WAS sent to help.
CELESTE
See! I knew it!
MARIE
I was sent to help clean. I'm from Merry
Maids.

CELESTE
I have a list of the things I need for my gris
Gris *(Pronounced GREE – GREE)* bag to break the
curse. One of those things is beads from a
voodoo priestess. Are you a voodoo priestess,
Marie?

MARIE
I'm just a St. Patrick's parishioner.

CELESTE
Close enough!...Do you have any beads Marie?

MARIE
I have my rosary.

CELESTE
I need it.

MARIE
It was my grandmother's.

CELESTE
I'll give you five hundred dollars for it.

*MARIE takes her rosary from her pocket and
thrusts it at CELESTE.*

MARY GRACE
Celeste, are you OK? I really do think she's
just a maid. Not that being a maid is not a
noble profession.

CELESTE
I believe she was sent here by the VooDoo
Queen, Marie Laveau. *(She studies Marie's eyes
closely)* Or she IS Marie Laveau, reincarnated
or something.

REGINA
Or...she's Marie... from Merry Maids.

CELESTE
I'm telling you. I've been in there meditating
and praying.

BREE
Honestly, Celeste, I find it hard to believe

that God would have sent you a voodoo queen to help in your hour of supposed need.

CELESTE

The Lord works in mysterious ways.

BREE

Not that mysterious. Although Mary was a maid.

CELESTE

I've got the list of things I need and better yet, I've got what I believe to be a reincarnated voodoo queen.

MARIE

I'm really just a good Catholic.

CELESTE

I've got some things to get and you're going with us Marie.

MARIE

What about the cleaning? Blaise will be mad.

CELESTE

You let me handle Blaise. We can clean it ourselves.

REGINA

Who is we? You and that mouse in your pocket? I'm not cleaning on vacation.

CELESTE

Whatever! We're going on a quest to cure this hex on me, and you, Marie, are coming with us!

MARIE

I can't. I have to clean an office tonight.

CELESTE

I'll give you another five hundred to come with us.

MARIE stands up quickly.

MARIE

I'm ready.

ACT TWO
Scene 7

*CATHERINE, MARY GRACE, BREE, AND REGINA are
seated. Each has in front of her a small glass
of green liquid. A spoon holding a sugar cube
is balanced and resting across the top of the
glass. A sign should read "Old Absinthe
House." CELESTE is sitting with MARIE at a
separate table in deep conversation. CELESTE
is holding a small note pad. THIBAUT enters.*

CELESTE
My, my, you sure get around.
THIBAUT
I could say the same thing about you.
CELESTE
I'm a tourist. I'm supposed to be getting
around. I need to cram in as much New Orleans
culture as I can.
THIBAUT
I live here.
CELESTE
Exactly, so do you always do this much cattin'
around?
THIBAUT
It is Mardi Gras, remember?
CELESTE
That's true. Listen, I'd love to chat, but
your friend the voodoo priestess at the ball
informed me I wasn't going to exist much
longer so I'm kind of busy here trying to do
all the things I can to break this curse
or whatever I got going on here.
THIBAUT
I thought you didn't believe that stuff.
CELESTE
Let's just say there were a few things I
couldn't explain away. I'm sorry but I've got

some things to gather before I go to the
graveyard.
THIBAUT
Graveyard?
CELESTE
I have to dig roots within six feet of Marie
Laveau's tomb at exactly midnight, so if
you'll excuse us. Oh by the way, this is
Marie, more than likely a reincarnated
voodoo priestess.
MARIE
I'm actually a Merry Maid. It's nice to meet
you.
THIBAUT
A Merry Maid?
CELESTE
Listen, we can't be here all night. And yes,
my life does depend on this, so I'll just say
I'm sorry in advance.

*Celeste takes each lady's drink, tosses aside
the spoon resting on top, and downs them one
by one. As soon as she turns up the last drink
the WAITER enters with a fancy bottle of
water.*

WAITER
(Very theatrically)
And now for the Absinthe Ritual. We will add
water, drop by drop, to create the louche.
Then we'll add the rest to dilute the Absinthe
perfectly.

*During the waiter's announcement Celeste is
gasping, blowing, gagging etc. from the
potency and taste of the absinthe. She might
grab one of the ladies' shirts or Thibaut's
shirt and try to wipe her tongue etc.*

THIBAUT
That was such a bad idea.
WAITER
Where is the..absinthe?
REGINA
Looks like we're gonna have to cut this ritual
short. We'll take the check.
WAITER
Hmph! Barbarians!

He saunters off with the water.

CELESTE
We have to go. I still have blue stones to
gather before we go to the graveyard to get
the roots.
MARY GRACE
Where in the world are we gonna find blue
stones?
MARIE
There are blue stones in an aquarium in the
lobby of an office building I clean.
CELESTE
And you ladies doubted me bringing Marie!

ACT TWO
Scene 8

*A sign says ST. LOUIS CEMETERY NO. 1. It's
dark. CELESTE is holding a flashlight and a
little bag. She is leading the way. MARY GRACE
is also holding a flashlight. MARY GRACE,
MARIE, REGINA, BREE, and CATHERINE are
stealthily following CELESTE.*

CELESTE
Listen. I don't want y'all to be jealous, but
that owl in front of us said that I was
looking good.
BREE
What?! What owl?
CELESTE
That owl, right in front of us. The one with
the tie-dyed T-shirt smoking a cigarette. I
know it's unhealthy, but somehow he makes it
look sexy.
CATHERINE
Celeste, in case you've forgotten, owls..
can't talk.
CELESTE
He can. Not only can he talk, he can dance
great. He's got some moves.

CELESTE begins to do a slow snaky dance.

MARY GRACE
Have you gone crazy?
CATHERINE
We should ask ourselves that, Mary Grace.
We're the ones following a crazy woman through
a cemetery in the middle of the night.
REGINA
That's right. We're just as crazy as she is
and none of us had a sip of that absinthe.

BREE
Yeah. At least she has an excuse.
REGINA
There are so many tombs here. How are we going
to figure out which one is Marie Laveau's?
MARY GRACE
This could take all night.
CELESTE
(wild and crazy) It can't take all night! I
have to dig the roots at midnight! We're going
to divide and conquer!
BREE
Oh hell no. We're not splitting up.
CELESTE
Oh yes we are! You and the other mermaids go
that way! The owl, the voodoo queen and I will
go this way! Come on Marie!

CELESTE and MARIE exit.

CATHERINE
Are we really going to do this?
MARY GRACE
Of course, we are. Celeste is convinced that
if she can get the last item for her gris gris
pouch that she can ward off this supposed
curse.
REGINA
Even if it's the nocebo effect, we've got to
go with it to help her.
CATHERINE
What on earth is the nocebo effect?
REGINA
A placebo effect is when you give somebody a
sugar pill and tell them it will help them and
they believe it, so it does. The nocebo effect
is when you tell somebody something will harm
them. They believe it so it eventually harms
them.

BREE

If Celeste really believes she's going to die
if she doesn't get all these things for her
voodoo bag of protection thing, she's gonna
freak out.

MARY GRACE

It's called a gris gris bag. I googled it.
She's only got the roots from around Marie
Laveau's tomb left to fill it and break the
curse.

CATHERINE

When we were in that VooDoo shop they had a
bunch of raccoon penises and chicken feet for
sale that were supposed to protect you and
bring you luck. I might not have any of that
handy-

BREE

Thank goodness.

CATHERINE

But I have this rabbit's foot. It's gotta be
as good as a chicken's foot.

MARY GRACE

Although maybe not as good as a raccoon penis.

CATHERINE

Anyway, here's hoping it's gonna protect us.
Celeste needs these roots so we're gonna by
God help her find them because she's our
friend.

REGINA

Catherine's right. I hope if I were high on
absinthe and determined to find a voodoo
queen's grave with a Merry Maid, y'all would
help me too.

BREE

I'm in.

REGINA

Let's go.

*REGINA, MARY GRACE, BREE, and CATHERINE exit.
CELESTE and MARIE enter. CELESTE falls to her
knees still clutching the little bag. MARIE is
holding the flashlight.*

CELESTE
(Wailing)
It's midnight! And I don't have my roots!
That's it! It's over! Celeste Abercrombie
Scarborough is a goner!
THIBAUT
(O.S.)
Celeste! Celeste!
CELESTE
Yes God! I'm ready!

*MARIE makes the sign of the cross.
THIBAUT enters. CELESTE stands.*

THIBAUT
Are you O.K.?
CELESTE
For now. Look Marie! Captain Kangaroo has come
to save us!

*MARIE stands between THIBAUT and CELESTE as
they face one another.*

THIBAUT
No. I'm THIBAUT, remember?
CELESTE
Yes! You are Thibaut! Regina calls you Thibaut
the Rodeo Cowboy! *(Celeste grinds the air and
pretends to swing a lasso above her head.)*
THIBAUT
Yeah? That Regina is a real doll.
CELESTE
She IS a doll! She's Baby Alive!

MARIE

I had one of those. They're kind of creepy.

CELESTE

Thibaut, I'm going to die soon. The voodoo priestess at The Bacchus Ball said that Celeste Abercrombie Scarborough was going to cease to exist soon. And Marie here, the supposed reincarnated voodoo queen, has been absolutely no help.

MARIE

I'm really just a Merry Maid.

CELESTE

I wasn't able to get any roots from near Marie Laveau's tomb. The place is covered in cement.

THIBAUT

Yeah, after Hurricane Katrina the city poured cement in all the cemeteries because a lot of the tombs floated away.

CELESTE

That's terrible!

THIBAUT

It was terrible.

CELESTE

It was really nice meeting you. I really would have liked to get to know you better. You're the only man I've been attracted to in five years.

THIBAUT

Well, maybe I can see if I can keep Celeste Abercrombie Scarborough around for a while.

CELESTE kisses THIBAUT.

ACT TWO
Scene 9

The flat. MARY GRACE enters wearing a wedding dress and looks out toward the audience and the fictitious cameraman.

MARY GRACE
Are we ready?... There's a bright reflection? Oh, that's just my big new ring…I came into some money and gifted myself.......Say something? I just said something.....Tell a joke? O.K... Two ladies were sitting on an airplane. The southern lady asked the snotty lady, where are you from? The snotty lady said, I'm from a place where we don't end our sentences in prepositions. So the southern lady said, I'm so sorry. Where are you from, bitch?.....O.K. we're ready now? Good. Welcome to a very special episode of Say Yes to Anything But a Wedding Dress. Today we go against the very grain of the show, but for a good reason.

CATHERINE, BREE, and REGINA enter wearing wedding dresses followed by BLAISE.

BLAISE
Today I introduce my line of wedding dresses and our new location, Ball Gowns AND Wedding Dresses by Blaise. But first, I'd like to introduce the couple that was the inspiration. Mr. and Mrs. Thibaut Boudreaux.

CELESTE and THIBAUT enter in wedding dress and tux jacket.

MARY GRACE
That's right, because Celeste Abercrombie
Scarborough...
MARY GRACE, REGINA, BREE, CATHERINE
Just doesn't exist anymore!!!
BLAISE
Don't you just love a happy ending? *(Gets
teary...)*

THE END

Made in the USA
Columbia, SC
22 September 2024

42046020R00054